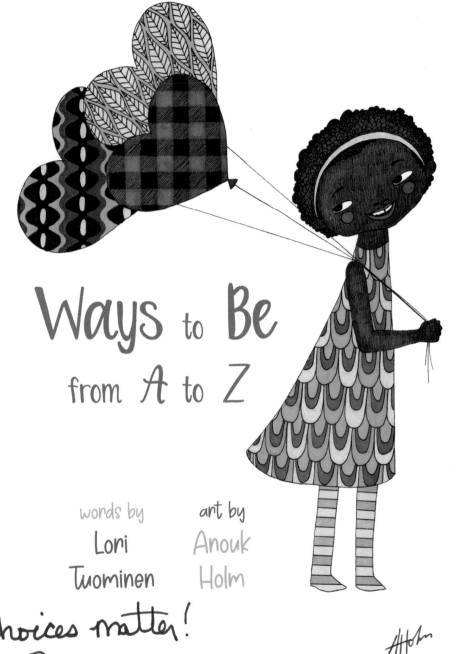

Ways to Be
from A to Z

words by
Lori Tuominen

art by
Anouk Holm

Your choices matter!
Lori Tuominen

INDIE OWL PRI

D1088014

Indie Owl Press Kids

4700 Millenia Blvd
Ste 175 #90776
Orlando, FL 32839

info@indieowlpress.com
IndieOwlPress.com

WAYS TO BE FROM A TO Z

www.waystobefromatoz.com

Book Design by NightOwlFreelance.com
Cover art by Anouk Holm

Hardback ISBN-13: 978-1-949193-79-4
Paperback ISBN-13: 978-1-949193-96-1

Printed in the U.S.A.

To my amazing family, I love you more than words can express. For those who are grown, I'm proud of how you've chosen to be in the world. And to Ailie, Elliott, and Ezra, may you always be curious, kind, helpful . . . and loving.

Be Adventurous

Be
Brave

Be

Curious

Be

Determined

Be
Forgiving

Be
Helpful

Be Imaginative

Be
Joyful

Be
Loving

Be
Nurturing

Be Observant

Be
Patient

Be Quirky

Be

Reflective

Be Silly

Be Trustworthy

Be Upbeat

Be Xenodochial

Be
Yourself

Be Zesty

Glossary

[glaw-suh-ree] – The place at the back of a book where words are defined.

Be [bee] – How you show up in the world; who you are, and how you act or behave. In every moment you have a choice of how you want to be, and your choice affects not only you but also everyone around you. Choose wisely!

Adventurous [ad-**ven**-cher-uhs] – Exploring new places; spending time doing activities that might be difficult or fun . . . or difficult *and* fun!

Brave [breyv] – Being afraid of something . . . and doing it anyway.

Curious [**kyoor**-ee-uhs] – Wanting to learn about everything! What are you curious about?

Determined [dih-**tur**-mind] – There's an old proverb, "If at first you don't succeed, try, try again." You seldom succeed on your first attempt at anything. Determined people keep trying!

Empathetic [em-puh-**thet**-ik] – Feeling what other people (or animals) are experiencing, and showing them care and compassion. This might include being a good listener when someone needs to talk, or just sitting quietly with them.

Forgiving [fer-**giv**-ing] – Letting go of what others have said or done to hurt you. Forgiving doesn't make it okay that someone hurt you. Forgiving helps you let go of the hurt.

Grateful [**greyt**-fuhl] – Feeling and expressing thanks. Appreciating what you have and who you are. This often (but not always) includes telling someone that you're grateful. Who or what are you grateful for today?

Helpful [**help**-fuhl] – Offering assistance to others, even if you don't receive anything back from them.

Imaginative [ih-**maj**-uh-nuh-tiv] – Pretending; playing out things you've thought about; using your imagination or being creative with your mind.

Joyful [**joi**-fuhl] – Having fun in the moment; experiencing happiness. You don't always feel this way, so when you do, celebrate!

Kind [kahynd] – Being nice to others. One thing to ask yourself is, "Would I like it if someone treated me this way?"

Loving [**luhv**-ing] – Feelings of warmth and affection toward others, such as a parent, sibling, friend, or pet. This could be expressed through a loving touch (like a hug), a kind gesture (like smiling), a statement such as "I love you," or "I really like you," or the feelings can simply live in your heart.

Mindful [**mahynd**-fuhl] – Being aware of each moment *as it is happening*; in other words, being aware of the *present* moment. What is happening right now; what do you notice?

Nurturing [**nur**-cher-ing] – Caring for others as well as for yourself. In what ways can you nurture yourself or others?

Observant [uhb-**zur**-vuhnt] – Noticing things you see, hear, smell, touch, taste, think, or feel; paying close attention to what is happening around you and inside you.

Patient [**pey**-shuhnt] – Being willing to wait. This might mean waiting for others or for something to happen.

Quirky [**kwur**-kee] – Embracing who you are and what you like to do, no matter how different you are from others!

Reflective [ri-**flek**-tiv] – Thinking about your life and learning from that process of looking closely. It's like looking at yourself in a mirror and studying who and what you see.

Silly [**sil**-ee] – Having fun; being goofy, playing.

Trustworthy [**truhst**-wur-thee] – Doing what you say you will do; being dependable; keeping your word. What can you do that will help people trust you?

Upbeat [**uhp**-beet] – Looking at the positive side of life and expressing it.

Vibrant [**vahy**-bruh nt] – Colorful; full of life.

Wise [wahyz] – Knowledgeable; sensible; showing good judgment. Learning from life experience (including challenges and mistakes— both yours and others'), so that you can make better choices in the future. We learn by noticing what works and also what doesn't.

Xenodochial [zee-nuh-**doh**-key-ul] – Friendly to strangers or new people. You can still be cautious, but you don't have to be afraid or unkind. This is the opposite of xenophobic, which means having a fear of strangers. How can you be friendly or welcoming to someone new?

Yourself [yohr-**self**] – Authentic. Who you are; not who your brother is or who your sister is, or who your mom wants you to be, or who your dad wants you to be. But who you truly are and who *you* want to be.

Zesty [**zes**-tee] – Live life fully! Enthusiastic.

The End

Pronunciations:

"Dictionary.com." Dictionary.com, 6 Dec. 2018, www.dictionary.com/.

"YourDictionary. The Way You Want It." YourDictionary.com, 6 Dec. 2018, www.yourdictionary.com/.

About the Author & Artist

Lori Tuominen is a coach and educator whose practice is steeped in positive ways of being. She has a Master's degree in Positive Organization Development and Change, a Certificate in Positive Psychology, and is a qualified Mindfulness-Based Stress Reduction (MBSR) teacher. She helps individual and organizational clients learn to flourish and thrive, to choose how they want to be in the world. She can be found trompsing around the hills of Western Massachusetts with her husband when they're not visiting Minnesota, where their four grown children and their families live. She's thrilled to have created this book with her daughter, Anouk Holm.

To learn more about Lori's work, please check out her website at **lorituominen.com**.

Anouk Holm is an illustrator, cartoonist, and writer. She lives in Minnesota with her husband and son. Her art can be found on Instagram **@anoukholm**.

Made in the USA
Lexington, KY
02 May 2019